Pa...

Fruit

by Marissa Kirkman

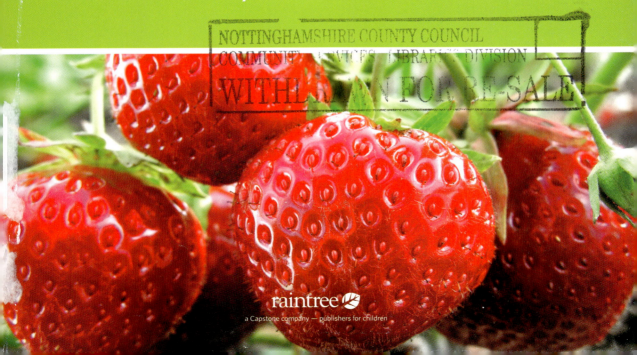

raintree 🍃
a Capstone company — publishers for children

Raintree is an imprint of Capstone Global Library Limited,
a company incorporated in England and Wales having its registered office at
264 Banbury Road, Oxford, OX2 7DY – Registered company number: 6695582

www.raintree.co.uk
myorders@raintree.co.uk

Edited by Erika L. Shores
Designed by Charmaine Whitman
Picture research by Svetlana Zhurkin
Production by Laura Manthe
Originated by Capstone Global Library
Printed and bound in India

ISBN 978 1 4747 8602 7 (hardback)
ISBN 978 1 4747 8608 9 (paperback)

British Library Cataloguing in Publication Data
A full catalogue record for this book is available from the British Library.

Acknowledgements
We would like to thank the following for permission to reproduce photographs: Shutterstock: Aaron Nystrom, 17, Alex S, 9 (inset), Alexander Raths, 21, aniad, 7 (top left), Anna Kucherova, 10, Chinnarit, 7 (top right), Chippo Medved, back cover left and throughout, Edward Lara, 20, guentermanaus, 19, Imagine Room, 1 (top), Iryna Koliadzynska, 7 (bottom right), janaph, 5, JCStudio, cover, Lano Lan, 13, LianeM, 9, Maryia Kazakova, 4, Nataly Studio, 16, Rudmer Zwerver, 15, TairA, 18, vincentchuls, 7 (bottom left), yevgeniy11, 11, yuris, 1 (bottom)

Every effort has been made to contact copyright holders of material reproduced in this book. Any omissions will be rectified in subsequent printings if notice is given to the publisher.

Contents

What is fruit?

Look at this plant. This plant grows flowers. The flowers turn into fruit.

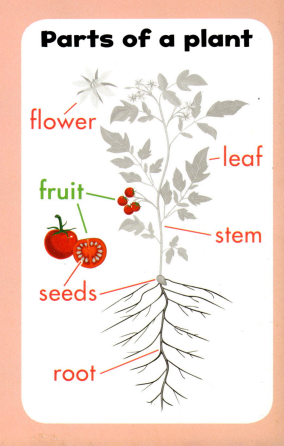

Parts of a plant

flower

leaf

fruit

stem

seeds

root

Fruit comes in many shapes and colours. It can be hard or soft. Some fruit is big. Some is small.

Fruit grows from some flowers.

Seeds are inside the fruit.

New plants grow from seeds.

kiwi plant

kiwi seeds

9

What does fruit do?

Fruit keeps seeds safe.

Some fruit is juicy.

Juice stops the seeds

from drying out.

pear seeds

Fruit helps seeds to move.

A coconut is a fruit.

It floats on water.

It carries the seed to land

where it can grow into a

new plant.

Animals eat fruit.

The seeds come out

when the animal poos.

They end up on the ground.

The seeds may grow into

new plants.

All kinds of fruit

Some nuts are fruit.

A pecan is a fruit.

It has a hard shell.

The seed is safe inside.

This is a star fruit.

If you cut it into slices

it looks like a star!

Look at all the fruit.
Fruit is tasty and good
for you too!

Glossary

flower   colourful part of a plant that makes fruit and seeds

fruit   fleshy, juicy part of a plant that contains seeds and can usually be eaten

juice   liquid part of a fruit

nut   dry, one-seeded fruit, such as an acorn, hazelnut or chestnut, that has a woody outer layer and does not break open when ripe

seed   part of a plant that will grow into a new plant

Find out more

A Look at Fruits (Parts of Plants), Lindsey Lowe
(Kidhaven Publishing, 2020)

Flowers and Plants of the British Isles (Let's Look At),
Lucy Beevor (Raintree, 2018)

Websites

BBC Bitesize: Plants
www.bbc.co.uk/bitesize/topics/zpxnyrd

Science Games for Kids: How Plants Grow
www.sciencekids.co.nz/gamesactivities/plantsgrow.html

Comprehension questions

1. How does the fruit help the seeds to move?

2. Which part of the plant turns into the fruit?

3. How many fruits can you name? Make a list.

Index

24